The Joy of
The Music of Love

**Serenades, Romances, Valentines, and many other
romantic musical offerings in easy piano arrangements
by Denes Agay.**

Cover design by Mike Bell Design, London

This book Copyright © 1999 by Yorktown Music Press, Inc.

All rights reserved. No part of this book may be
reproduced in any form or by any electronic or mechanical means,
including information storage and retrieval systems,
without permission in writing from the publisher.

Order No. YK 21818
US International Standard Book Number: 0.8256.8100.6
UK International Standard Book Number: 0.7119.6759.8

Exclusive Distributors:
Music Sales Corporation
257 Park Avenue South, New York, NY 10010 USA
Music Sales Limited
8/9 Frith Street, London W1V 5TZ England
Music Sales Pty. Limited
120 Rothschild Street, Rosebery, Sydney, NSW 2018, Australia

Printed in the United States of America by
Vicks Lithograph and Printing Corporation

Yorktown Music Press, Inc.
New York/London/Sydney

Contents

I Love You

Edvard Grieg

Copyright © 1999 by Yorktown Music Press, Inc. (ASCAP)
International Copyright Secured. All Rights Reserved.

Theme from "Romeo and Juliet"
(Version I)

Peter I. Tchaikovsky

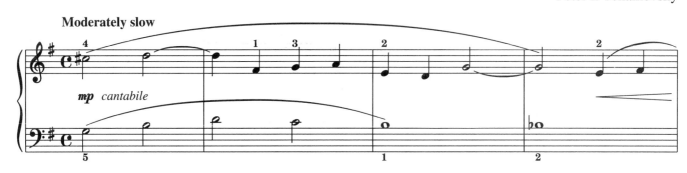

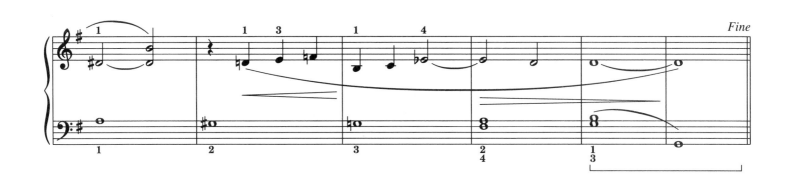

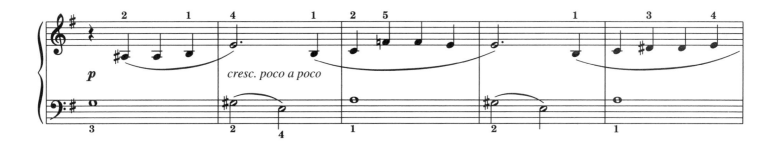

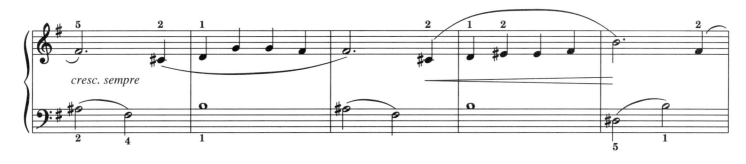

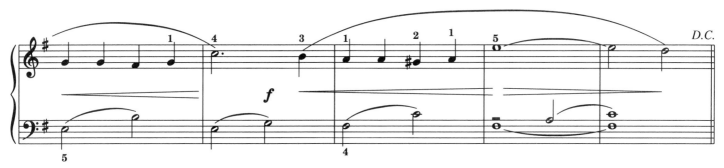

Copyright © 1999 by Yorktown Music Press, Inc. (ASCAP)
International Copyright Secured. All Rights Reserved.

Theme from Romeo and Juliet
(Version II)

Peter I. Tchaikovsky

Copyright © 1999 by Yorktown Music Press, Inc. (ASCAP)
International Copyright Secured. All Rights Reserved.

Romance

Anton Rubinstein

Copyright © 1999 by Yorktown Music Press, Inc. (ASCAP)
International Copyright Secured. All Rights Reserved.

Notturno
from String Quartet No. 2

Alexander Borodin

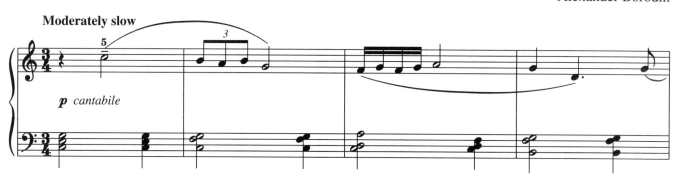

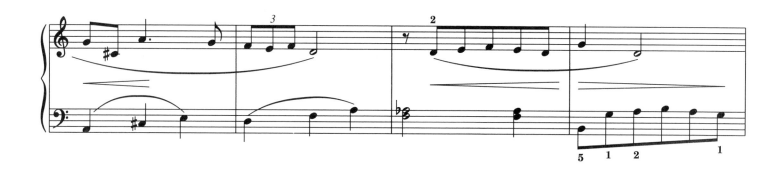

Copyright © 1999 by Yorktown Music Press, Inc. (ASCAP)
International Copyright Secured. All Rights Reserved.

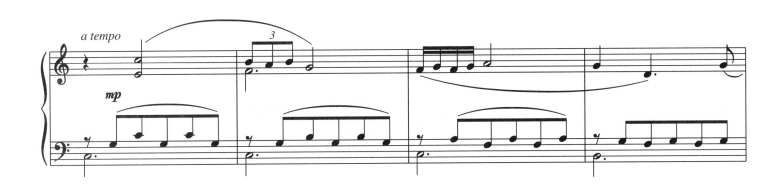

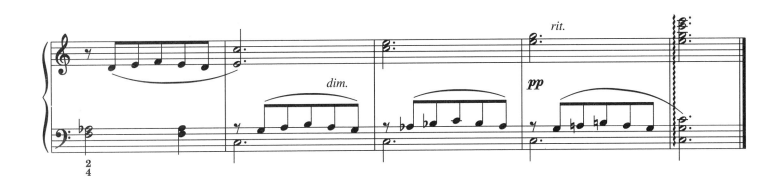

Liebestraum Waltz

Franz Liszt

Copyright © 1999 by Yorktown Music Press, Inc. (ASCAP)
International Copyright Secured. All Rights Reserved.

Serenade

Franz Schubert

Copyright © 1999 by Yorktown Music Press, Inc. (ASCAP)
International Copyright Secured. All Rights Reserved.

Romance

from The Pearl Fishers

Georges Bizet

Copyright © 1999 by Yorktown Music Press, Inc. (ASCAP)
International Copyright Secured. All Rights Reserved.

Theme from "The Magic Flute"

Dies Bildniss Ist Bezaubernd Schön

Wolfgang Amadeus Mozart

Copyright © 1999 by Yorktown Music Press, Inc. (ASCAP)
International Copyright Secured. All Rights Reserved.

Salut d'Amour
(Love's Greeting)

Edward Elgar

Copyright © 1999 by Yorktown Music Press, Inc. (ASCAP)
International Copyright Secured. All Rights Reserved.

Romanza
from "Eine Kleine Nachtmusik"

Wolfgang Amadeus Mozart

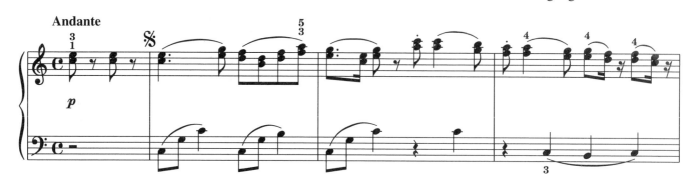

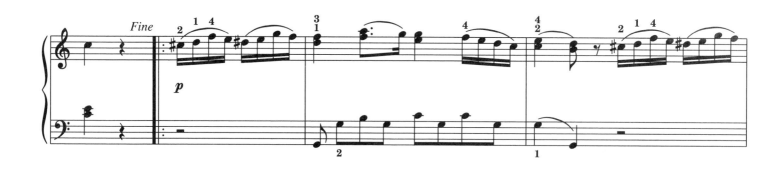

Copyright © 1999 by Yorktown Music Press, Inc. (ASCAP)
International Copyright Secured. All Rights Reserved.

Remembrance Waltz

Andantino grazioso

John Field

Copyright © 1999 by Yorktown Music Press, Inc. (ASCAP)
International Copyright Secured. All Rights Reserved.

19

Dedication
(Widmung)

Jean Reynolds Davis

Robert Schumann

Lively, fervent

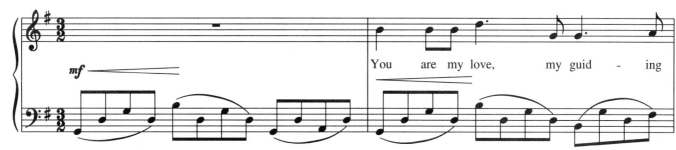

You are my love, my guid - ing

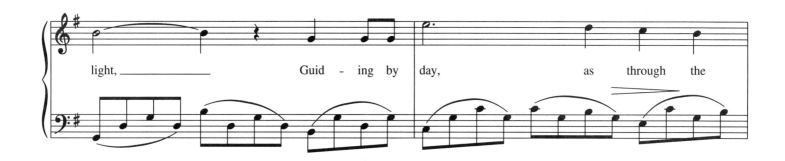

light, _____ Guid - ing by day, as through the

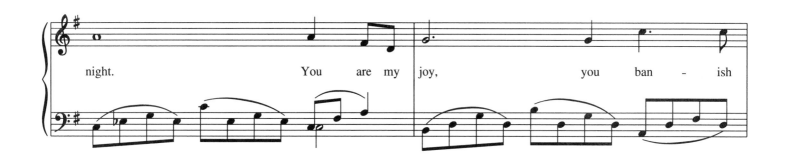

night. You are my joy, you ban - ish

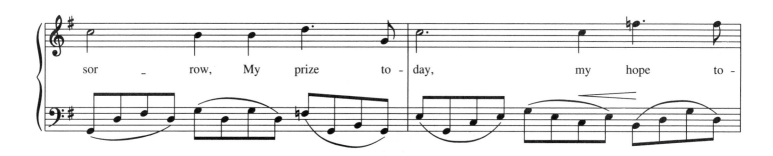

sor - row, My prize to - day, my hope to -

Copyright © 1999 by Yorktown Music Press, Inc. (ASCAP)
International Copyright Secured. All Rights Reserved.

Nocturne
from "A Midsummer Night's Dream"

Felix Mendelssohn

Copyright © 1999 by Yorktown Music Press, Inc. (ASCAP)
International Copyright Secured. All Rights Reserved.

Impatience

from the song "Ungeduld"

Franz Schubert

Copyright © 1999 by Yorktown Music Press, Inc. (ASCAP)
International Copyright Secured. All Rights Reserved.

Open Thy Heart

Ouvre Ton Coeur

Georges Bizet

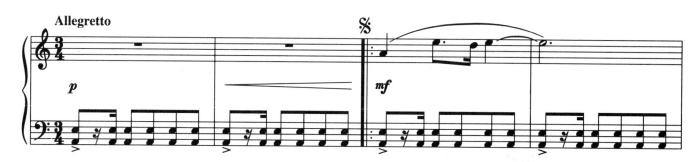

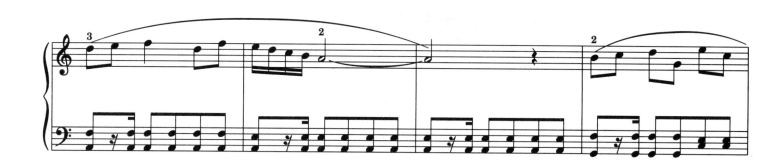

Copyright © 1999 by Yorktown Music Press, Inc. (ASCAP)
International Copyright Secured. All Rights Reserved.

Bonjour, Suzon

Leo Delibes

Copyright © 1999 by Yorktown Music Press, Inc. (ASCAP)
International Copyright Secured. All Rights Reserved.

Who Dreamed Up This Ditty?

Wer Hat Dies Liedlein Erdacht

Gustav Mahler

* *About the lovely innkeeper's daughter with dark brown eyes and rosy lips.*

Copyright © 1999 by Yorktown Music Press, Inc. (ASCAP)
International Copyright Secured. All Rights Reserved.

Themes from "Madame Butterfly"

Giacomo Puccini

Copyright © 1999 by Yorktown Music Press, Inc. (ASCAP)
International Copyright Secured. All Rights Reserved.

Serenata

from "Pagliacci"

Ruggero Leoncavallo

Copyright © 1999 by Yorktown Music Press, Inc. (ASCAP)
International Copyright Secured. All Rights Reserved.

Madamoiselle! Monsieur!

from "Manon"

Jules Massenet

Andante cantabile

Copyright © 1999 by Yorktown Music Press, Inc. (ASCAP)
International Copyright Secured. All Rights Reserved.

My Heart at Thy Sweet Voice

from "Samson and Delilah"

Camille Saint-Saëns

Moderately slow

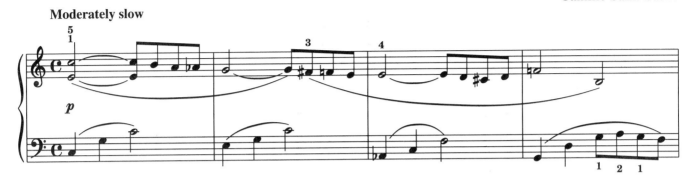

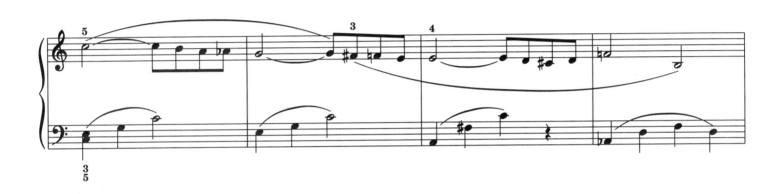

Copyright © 1999 by Yorktown Music Press, Inc. (ASCAP)
International Copyright Secured. All Rights Reserved.

Oh, Night of Love

from "Faust"

Charles Gounod

Copyright © 1999 by Yorktown Music Press, Inc. (ASCAP)
International Copyright Secured. All Rights Reserved.

I Have a Song

from "The Yeomen of the Guard"

William S. Gilbert

Arthur Sullivan

Copyright © 1999 by Yorktown Music Press, Inc. (ASCAP)
International Copyright Secured. All Rights Reserved.

It Must Be Wonderful

Es Muss Ein Wunderbares Sein

Franz Liszt

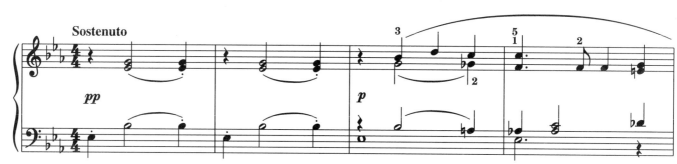

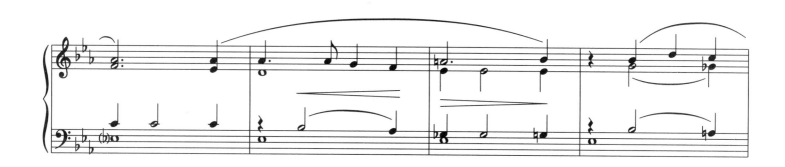

Copyright © 1999 by Yorktown Music Press, Inc. (ASCAP)
International Copyright Secured. All Rights Reserved.

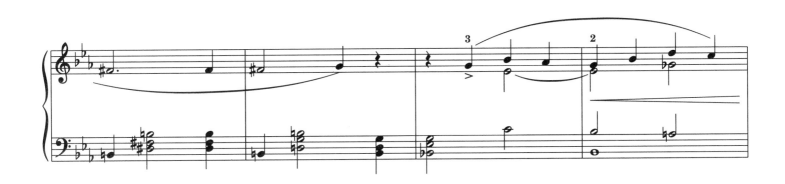

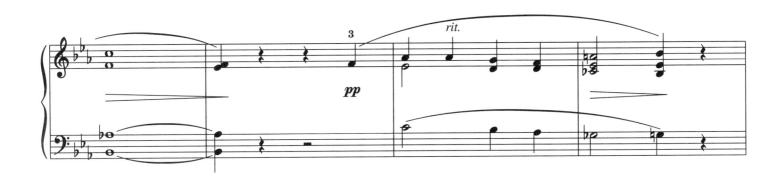

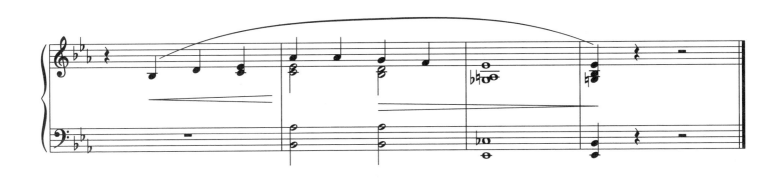

The Flower Song
from "Carmen"

Georges Bizet

Copyright © 1999 by Yorktown Music Press, Inc. (ASCAP)
International Copyright Secured. All Rights Reserved.

Dedication
Zueignung

Richard Strauss

Copyright © 1999 by Yorktown Music Press, Inc. (ASCAP)
International Copyright Secured. All Rights Reserved.

For You, My Love

Sidney Leif

Denes Agay

Copyright © 1999 by Yorktown Music Press, Inc. (ASCAP)
International Copyright Secured. All Rights Reserved.

sing.   Can it be true,   you're stand-ing here be-

side me, _____ A dream like you   will take my hand and

guide me. _____ So from this day   when we de-clare "I

do," _____   Through all e-ter-ni-ty _____ I prom-ise

you, _____   Un-til the day death us do

In the Garden

from "Rustic Wedding Symphony"

Karl Goldmark

Copyright © 1999 by Yorktown Music Press, Inc. (ASCAP)
International Copyright Secured. All Rights Reserved.

Serenata Argentina
(Ay, Ay, Ay)

Traditional

Copyright © 1999 by Yorktown Music Press, Inc. (ASCAP)
International Copyright Secured. All Rights Reserved.

Valentine Greeting

(Based on the song "Gruss")

Felix Mendelssohn

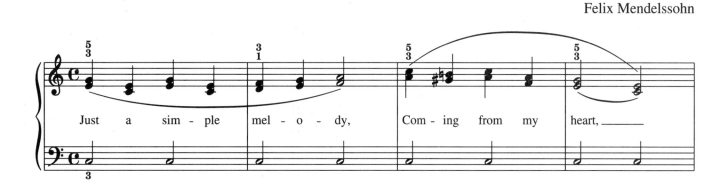

Just a sim - ple mel - o - dy, Com - ing from my heart, ____

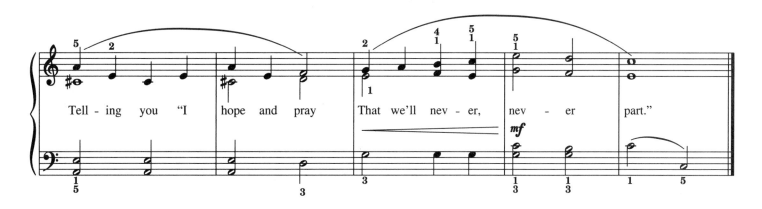

Tell - ing you "I hope and pray That we'll nev - er, nev - er part."

Copyright © 1999 by Yorktown Music Press, Inc. (ASCAP)
International Copyright Secured. All Rights Reserved.

First Love

Old Hungarian Serenade

Jozsef Kossovits

* This famous melody was until recently attributed to János Lavotta (1764–1820)

Copyright © 1999 by Yorktown Music Press, Inc. (ASCAP)
International Copyright Secured. All Rights Reserved.

53

Love's Joy

Liebesfreud

Fritz Kreisler

Copyright © 1999 by Yorktown Music Press, Inc. (ASCAP)
International Copyright Secured. All Rights Reserved.

Intermezzo
(A Love Story)

Heinz Provost

Copyright © 1936 (Renewed) by Music Sales Corporation (ASCAP)
International Copyright Secured. All Rights Reserved.

Amoureuse
(Valse Continentale)

Rudolphe Berger

Copyright © 1999 by Yorktown Music Press, Inc. (ASCAP)
International Copyright Secured. All Rights Reserved.

For Mary

A Golden Valentine

Denes Agay

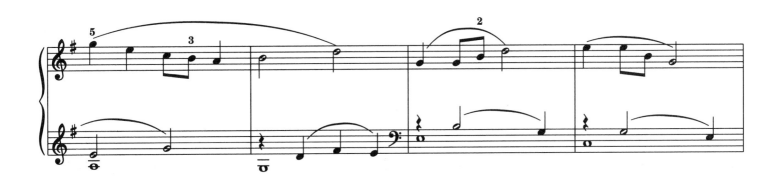

Copyright © 1998 by Yorktown Music Press, Inc. (ASCAP)
International Copyright Secured. All Rights Reserved.

O Whistle and I'll Come to You

Scotch folk song

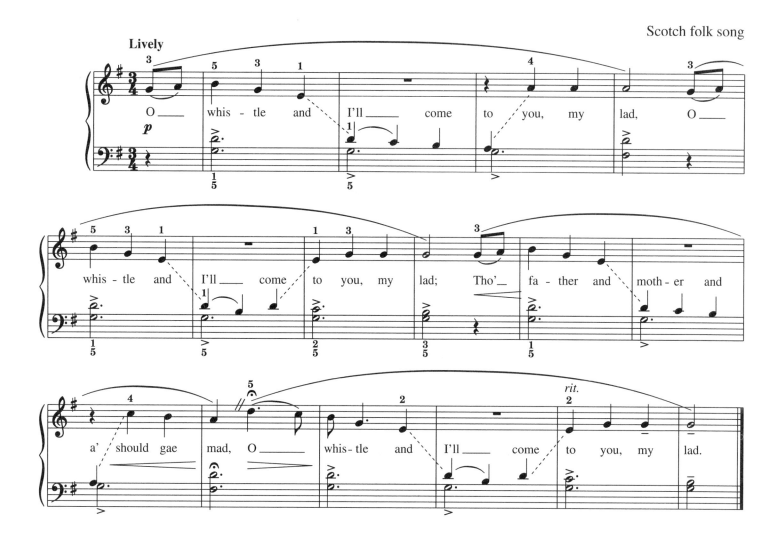

Who Will Shoe Your Pretty Little Foot

American folk song

Copyright © 1999 by Yorktown Music Press, Inc. (ASCAP)
International Copyright Secured. All Rights Reserved.

Black Is the Color
Of My True Love's Hair

American folk song

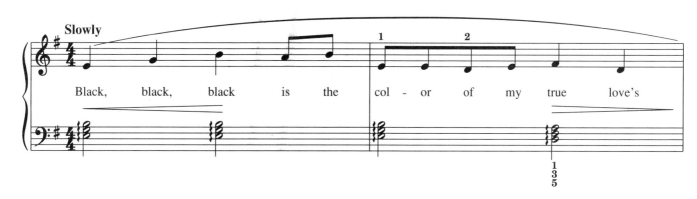

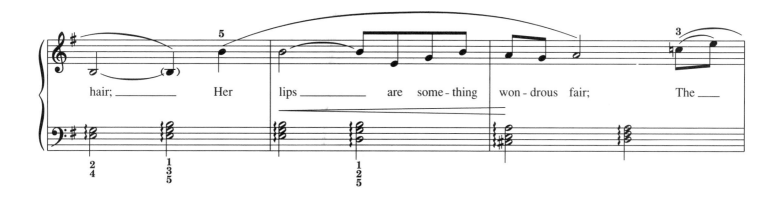

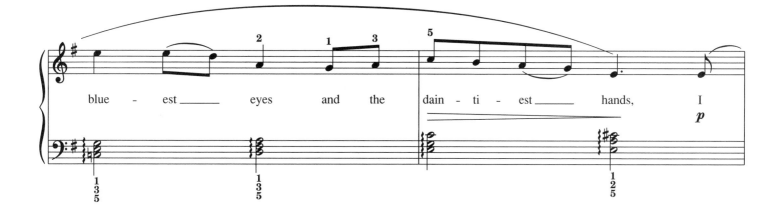

Copyright © 1999 by Yorktown Music Press, Inc. (ASCAP)
International Copyright Secured. All Rights Reserved.

I Know My Love

Irish folk song

Copyright © 1999 by Yorktown Music Press, Inc. (ASCAP)
International Copyright Secured. All Rights Reserved.

My One and Only Love

Hungarian folk song

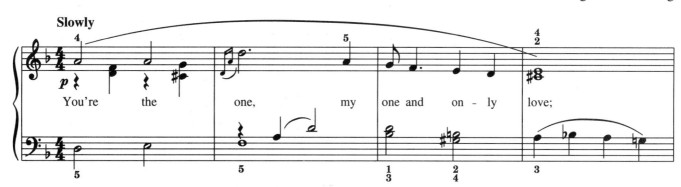

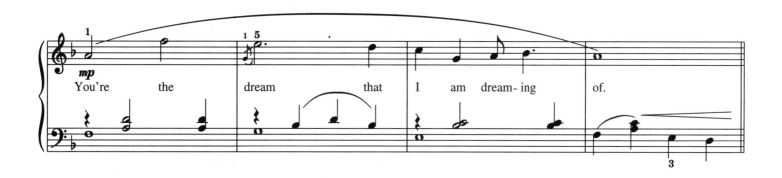

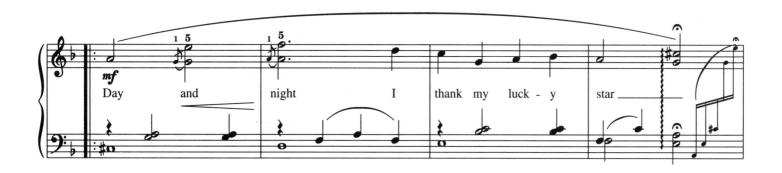

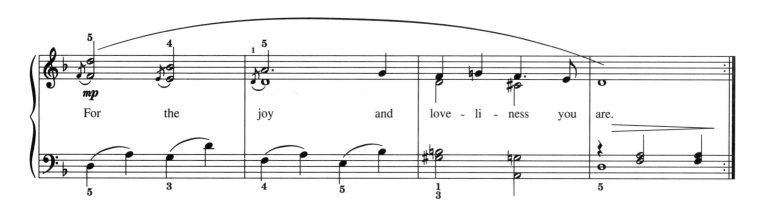

Copyright © 1999 by Yorktown Music Press, Inc. (ASCAP)
International Copyright Secured. All Rights Reserved.

Auprès de ma Blonde

French folk song

Comfortable, lilting tempo

Copyright © 1999 by Yorktown Music Press, Inc. (ASCAP)
International Copyright Secured. All Rights Reserved.

Melody of Love

H. Engelmann

Copyright © 1999 by Yorktown Music Press, Inc. (ASCAP)
International Copyright Secured. All Rights Reserved.

Fascination

Moderate waltz tempo

F. D. Marchetti

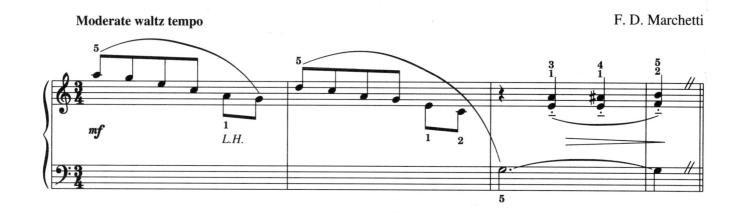

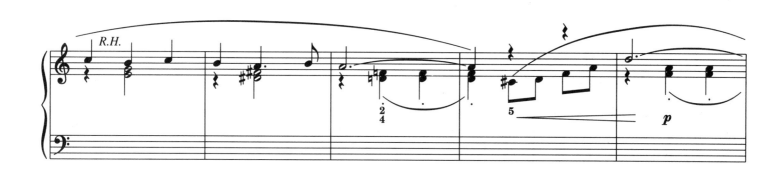

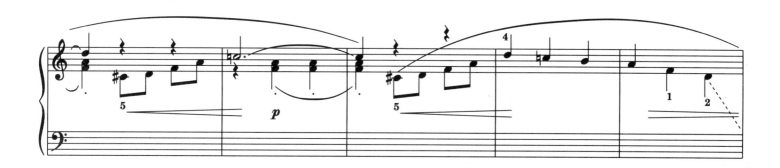

Copyright © 1999 by Yorktown Music Press, Inc. (ASCAP)
International Copyright Secured. All Rights Reserved.

Will You Remember

from "Sweetheart"

Sigmund Romberg

Copyright © 1999 by Yorktown Music Press, Inc. (ASCAP)
International Copyright Secured. All Rights Reserved.

When You Were Sweet Sixteen

James Thornton

Copyright © 1999 by Yorktown Music Press, Inc. (ASCAP)
International Copyright Secured. All Rights Reserved.

A Pretty Girl Is Like a Melody

Irving Berlin

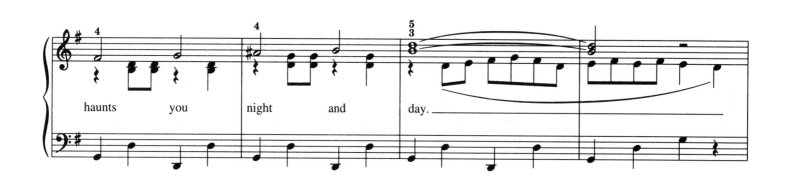

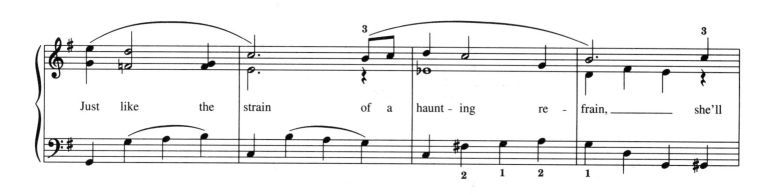

Copyright © 1999 by Yorktown Music Press, Inc. (ASCAP)
International Copyright Secured. All Rights Reserved.

They Didn't Believe Me

Herbert Reynolds

Jerome Kern

Andante moderato

And when I told them _____ how won-der-ful you are,

_____ They did-n't be - lieve me, _____ they did-n't be - lieve me! _____

_____ Your lips, your eyes, your cheeks, your hair are in a

class be - yond com - pare, You're the love - li - est girl _____

_____ that one could see! _____ And when I tell them, _____

Copyright © 1999 by Yorktown Music Press, Inc. (ASCAP)
International Copyright Secured. All Rights Reserved.

If You Were the Only Girl

Clifford Grey

Nat D. Ayer

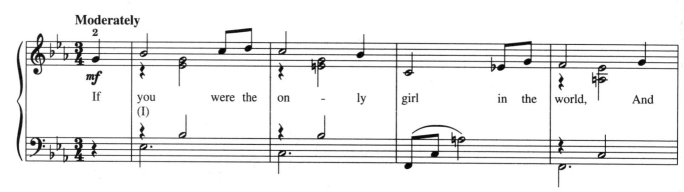

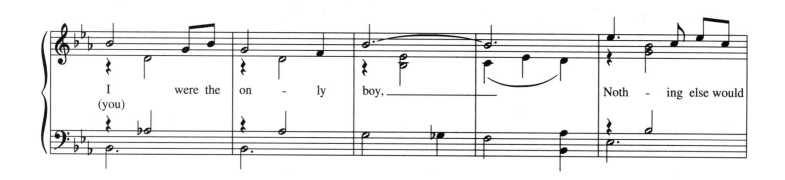

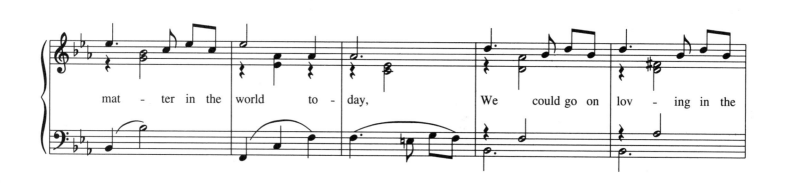

Copyright © 1999 by Yorktown Music Press, Inc. (ASCAP)
International Copyright Secured. All Rights Reserved.

Poem

Zdenko Fibich

Copyright © 1999 by Yorktown Music Press, Inc. (ASCAP)
International Copyright Secured. All Rights Reserved.